10 9 8 7 6 5 4 3 2

Manufactured in China, September 2023
This product conforms to CPSIA 2008

Library of Congress Cataloging-in-Publication Data is available on file.

Cover design by Elke Kohlmann and Daniel Brount
Cover illustration by Dagmar Geisler

Print ISBN: 978-1-5107-4660-2
Ebook ISBN: 978-1-5107-4671-8

If I Get Lost

Stay Put, Remain Calm, and Ask for Help

Written and Illustrated by
Dagmar Geisler

Translated by
Andrea Jones Berasaluce

Sky Pony Press
New York

Lu and Mama are going into town. They want to buy bread, bananas, and red-and-white striped socks for Lu. They desperately need these things.

There's a lot going on at the marketplace today.

"I hope you don't get lost in this crowd," Mama says.

"I won't get lost," says Lu.

The sidewalks are cramped, and Lu can only see people's legs.

Luckily, Mama is wearing her red coat. It is so eye-catching that it's impossible to miss.

A boy is standing by the fruit stand. He doesn't look very happy.

"Are you lost?" asks Lu.

"Of course not!" says the boy.

At the bread stand, the crowd is even worse. People push and shove. "It's too bad I'm so small," Lu thinks.

But then someone even smaller than Lu runs over. "You're so sweet," says Lu. The little dog wags its tail.

As Lu and Mama walk on, the dog runs along with them. Sometimes he runs ahead, sometimes to the right, and sometimes to the left. Lu doesn't let him out of her sight.

"Look what sweet company we have!" Lu exclaims. But the sounds of the market are so loud that Mama doesn't hear her. Lu tugs at Mama's coat. "Look!"

The woman who turns around definitely isn't Mama. Scared,
Lu turns in every direction. Mama is nowhere to be seen.

"See, now you're lost, too," says someone in a sad voice.

"So you *are* lost," says Lu. "Why did you lie to me?"

Instead of answering, the boy asks, "What do we now?"

"First rule of being lost: keep still and shout! If there's something on which you can stand a little bit higher, climb on it and yell! It's best not to move from that spot, so your parents can better find you."

"Uh huh," says the boy and wipes the tears from his eyes. He doesn't sound very convinced. "What if no one looks for you?"

"All parents look for their lost kids," says Lu.

"Even if you were bad before?" asks the boy.

"Of course," says Lu. "Parents always want to get their children back."

"Even if they're terribly mad at you?"

"Even then," says Lu.

"Phew," says the boy, relieved. "But I think that staying here and shouting isn't helping me at all."

"Why not?"

"I've already been here a while and run here and there, but Papa's nowhere to be seen. I'm sure we'll never find each other again."

"Nonsense," says Lu.

"It begins with 01 . . .   and then 50 . . . or 60?

There's also a 7 and a 3.   Oh no, oh no, oh no, it's not coming to me!

"It's all over now. I know it! I'll never get back home."

"Nonsense," says Lu.

"Rule number two: if you can't find each other, call them!"

Lu climbs down from the crate. "We'll ask someone to call your father. Your dad does have a cell phone with him, right?"

"Of course!" The boy nods.

"Do you know the number? I have our address on a piece of paper, but Mama always plays it safe and that's why I have our number here on my arm."

The boy laughs. "I know Dad's number by heart. I'm not a baby anymore.

"Rule number three: if none of this works, we call the police."

"The police?" shouts the boy. "I haven't committed any crimes!"

"No, silly," Lu says. "The police aren't only there to catch criminals. The police are also there to help us."

"Really?" asks the boy.

"Of course," says Lu. "Now we just need someone who can call them for us."

But that's easier said than done. Lu asks a man, but he has headphones on his ears and can't hear her at all. Then a woman answers her in a totally foreign language. At the fishmonger's, Lu has a breakthrough. "I have a cell phone, but we can't call from here; it's too loud. Come with me to my car. It will work better from there."

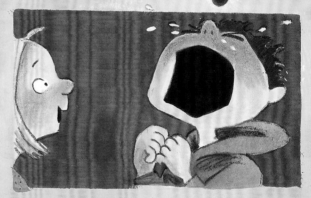

"No, thank you!" says Lu pleasantly. "I don't know you, so I can't go with you!"

"Are you crazy?" exclaims the boy once the fishmonger has gone away.

"Not at all!" says Lu. "That's rule number four: even if I'm lost, I never go with just anyone."

"What about me? Should I go sleep under a bridge, then?"

"Nonsense," says Lu.

"Now we've come to rule number five: if I need to get help, I go to a place where there are as many people as possible and where someone can clearly see me."

"How about the pharmacy?" asks the boy.

"Good idea," says Lu.

Ding-dong goes the doorbell as the two of them enter the shop.

"Good afternoon," Lu says to the pharmacist. "We're both lost. Could you perhaps call my mother? And the police, too, please."

"Do you have your mother's number?" asks the pharmacist kindly.

"Yes, I do. But we need the police first. He . . ." Lu turns around. "What's your name, by the way?"

"Roberto," says the boy.

"Roberto has been lost for much longer than I have."

"Well then," says the pharmacist and picks up the phone.

The police arrive very quickly. They were close by, eating lunch. The pharmacist is just about to dial Mama's number when someone else rushes into the store. It's an older girl and she is very upset.

"Have you seen a little dog?" she asks.

"Yes, I have!"
Lu wants to
call out, but
then a man
comes running
inside. He is even
more upset than the girl.
His face is red as a tomato.

"Have you seen a little
boy?" he shouts.

"Papa!" yells Roberto.

The pharmacy is now packed. One of the policemen coaxes the little dog into the store using the rest of his lunch. The pharmacist is finally about to dial Mama's number, but it is now awfully loud.

So loud that Lu almost doesn't hear the *ding-dong* of the shop door.

"Lu!" exclaims Mama. She rushes in and hugs her daughter so tightly that Lu almost can't breathe, and then Mama cries, too.

"But Mama!" says Lu. "Remember rule number six when lost: don't panic!"

"It's true!" sniffs Mama. "I was afraid that you had forgotten everything we'd discussed about getting lost."

"Not at all!" says Roberto. "She hasn't. She knows it all perfectly."

When I Get Lost: Rules For Children

 I stay where I am. My parents are looking for me. This way, they can find me more easily. (If we have picked a meeting place, I go there. The meeting place must be easy to find, and it must be easy to recognize one another when there.)

 I ask someone to call my parents. I have the number with me. (The most important thing is not to lose it.)

 If this doesn't work, someone can also call the police.

 I never go anywhere with anyone to make a call.

 If I can't find anyone to call for me, then I go somewhere everyone can see me. For example, into a business.

 I don't panic. If I stay calm, I can think things through better.

Ideas for Parents

For Point 1: You can set a meeting point at a straightforward location. Some examples of good, visible places are fountains, a flagpole, or something similar, or pick a site at a marketplace, a building on a train platform, or a large play structure on a playground. In any case, it should be a point the child can reach safely and quickly. For larger outings, it is better to pick a meeting place than to not.

For Point 2: You can place your cell phone number in the child's pocket, but s/he might still lose it. It is better to put it in a pouch around his/her neck. A phone number on their arm is perhaps not so pretty, but in any case, it is a good idea for the child's safety.

For Point 3: Practice the number for the police (911) and emergency services with your child. This can be done in a fun way.

For Point 4: Talk with your child before an outing about whom to call in case of emergency. In addition to the police, it can be train or flight crews, or people whom you personally trust. It is important that the number of people is manageable, so the child doesn't get easily confused.

For Point 5: Here, too, it makes sense to talk about such places beforehand. For example, you can take a walk through the city to point out suitable places from time to time.

For Point 6: The better a child is prepared for a difficult situation, the less likely s/he is to panic. The same goes for you! ☺